Countries Around the World

North Korea

Elizabeth Raum

Heinemann Library
Chicago, Illinois

www.capstonepub.com
Visit our website to find out more information about Heinemann-Raintree books.

To order:
☎ Phone 888-454-2279
💻 Visit www.capstonepub.com
to browse our catalog and order online.

Edited by Abby Colich and Claire Throp
Designed by Ryan Frieson and Steven Mead
Original illustrations © Capstone Global Library, Ltd., 2012
Illustrated by Oxford Designers & Illustrators
Picture research by Ruth Blair
Originated by Capstone Global Library, Ltd.
Printed in China by China Translation and Printing Services

15 14 13 12 11
10 9 8 7 6 5 4 3 2 1

Library of Congress Cataloging-in-Publication Data
Raum, Elizabeth.
  North Korea / Elizabeth Raum.
    p. cm.—(Countries around the world)
  Includes bibliographical references and index.
  ISBN 978-1-4329-6107-7 (hb)—ISBN 978-1-4329-6133-6 (pb)
  1. Korea (North)—Juvenile literature. I. Title.
  DS932.R38 2012
  951.93—dc22   2011015433

Acknowledgments
The author and publishers are grateful to the following for permission to reproduce copyright material: Alamy p. 33 (© amana images inc.); Corbis pp. 7 (© Reinhard Krause/Reuters), 13 (© Kim Kyung-Hoon/Reuters), 14 (© Kim Chul-Soo/epa), 16 (© Wu Hong/epa), 18, 39 (© STRINGER/KOREA/Reuters), 22 (© STF/epa), 23 (© Keren Su), 24 (© Miguel Toran/epa), 26 (© kcna/Xinhua Press), 27 (© DAVID GRAY/Reuters), 28 (© Alain Nogues), 30 (© Lee Jae-Won/Reuters), 31 (© David Gray/Reuters), 32 (© JEON HEON-KYUN/epa), 34 (© JO YONG-HAK/Reuters), 36 (John Sun/epa); Dreamstime.com p. 5 (© Linqong); Getty Images pp. 10 (Keystone-France/Gamma-Keystone), 25 (Alexander Hassenstein), 35 (Menahem Kahana/AFP); Photolibrary p. 8 (Tony Waltham); Shutterstock pp. 21 (© zschnepf), 46 (© pdesign).

Cover photograph of the Tower of Juche, Pyongyang, North Korea reproduced with permission of Photolibrary (Tony Waltham/Robert Harding Travel).

We would like to thank Jennifer Jung-Kim for her invaluable help in the preparation of this book.

Every effort has been made to contact copyright holders of any material reproduced in this book. Any omissions will be rectified in subsequent printings if notice is given to the publisher.

Note on Romanization of Korean

McCune-Reischauer is the Romanization method preferred by academics. This is a phonetic system that reflects Korean pronunciation. But some people find this system difficult because it takes time to learn.

Since 2000, the South Korean government has been using a different system that is easier to learn. North Korea uses yet another method of Romanization that also has numerous exceptions, but it is not used in this book except where the name or term is commonly known in the West (for example, Kim Il Sung, Kim Jong Il, Juche).

This book primarily uses the South Korean system except when names are more commonly spelled in a different way (for example, Syngman Rhee and Kim Il Sung). The McCune-Reischauer system is given in parentheses after the first use of the South Korean system.

Contents

Some words in the book are in bold, **like this**. You can find out what they mean by looking in the glossary.

Introducing North Korea

North Korea is officially called the Democratic People's **Republic** of Korea (DPRK). This country occupies the northern half of the Korean **Peninsula**. North and South Korea are separated by an **artificial** boundary called the **Demilitarized Zone (DMZ)**. The East Sea lies to the east. The Yellow Sea lies to the west. China and Russia form the northern border. North Korea has a total area of 46,540 square miles (120,538 square kilometers). That is slightly smaller than the state of Mississippi.

Land of mystery

Much about life in modern North Korea remains a mystery. This is because North Korea is one of the most **isolated** countries in the world. The North Korean government allows few outsiders to visit. Visitors must agree to travel with a North Korean official. The official, called a "minder," decides where visitors can go, what they can photograph, and whom they can meet. Foreign television crews and reporters rarely visit North Korea. North Koreans rarely travel to other countries. Most North Koreans do not have cell phones or access to the Internet, so they do not contact family and friends overseas.

Daily Life

Koreans greet one another with a simple bow. Children bow to their parents, teachers, and leaders. In North Korea, pictures of the current leader, Kim Jong Il, and his father, Kim Il Sung, are displayed in homes, public buildings, and on outdoor posters. Children and adults bow before these pictures as a sign of respect.

Many ancient buildings, such as this one built in 1042, still exist throughout North Korea.

History: The Hermit Kingdom

The **ancestors** of today's Koreans came from Asia sometime between 8,000 and 4,000 BCE. They lived along rivers and coasts, and they used polished stones as tools and weapons. Around 3,000 BCE, others arrived from Manchuria, Mongolia, and southern Siberia. They built walled towns, raised animals, and introduced weaving.

Early kingdoms

The walled towns became powerful kingdoms. North Koreans believe that the Korean nation began in 2333 BCE. At that time, a king named Dangun (also called Tangun) founded the Old Joseon (also called Old Choson) Kingdom, near present-day Pyongyang. This was a very powerful kingdom. By 300 BCE, Joseon warriors rode horses and used iron weapons to fight neighboring Chinese kingdoms. In 108 BCE, China's Han **Dynasty** (206 BCE–220 CE) moved south and took control of Korea. Chinese **culture** influenced life on the Korean **Peninsula**. At this time, Korean farmers began growing rice.

Eventually, people living along the northwest border challenged the Han Dynasty. The Korean kingdom of Goguryeo (also called Koguryo) was founded in 37 BCE. The city of Lolang (near present-day Pyongyang) became the capital in 370 CE. Two other kingdoms—Silla and Baekje (also called Paekche)—joined Goguryeo in ruling Korea.

DANGUN

According to legend, Dangun was the child of a bear who had become human. His father was Hwanung, the God of All and Ruler of Heaven. Dangun became a wise and powerful leader. Legend claims that he died at the age of 1,908 and became a mountain god. The North Korean government recently claimed to have found Dangun's grave.

Rice growing began during China's Han Dynasty rule. These workers are harvesting rice in fields just outside the North Korean capital of Pyongyang.

This is the tomb of King Kongmin (also called Gongmin), who ruled during the Goryeo Dynasty, from 1351 until 1374.

Later kingdoms

In 668 CE, the Later Silla Dynasty took control. Silla kings ruled for about 250 years. In 918 the Goryeo (also called Koryo) Dynasty took over. Goryeo kings traded gold and silver with China for beautiful silks and porcelain. Despite many challenges from the Mongols (people from Mongolia) and Japanese, the Goryeo Dynasty lasted nearly 500 years. The English word *Korea* comes from the native Korean word *Goryeo*.

In 1392 the new Joseon Dynasty took control. Joseon kings extended Korea's borders to the north. The arts flourished. So did science and medicine. In 1446 the Korean alphabet, the Hangeul (also called Hangul), was created.

A strict class system developed, with the king at the top and an educated class, called the *yangban*, next in importance. Farmers, fishermen, and workers followed. Slaves were last.

After invasions from Japan (1592–1598) and Manchuria (1627–1636), Korean rulers limited trade with other nations. Korea became known as the **Hermit** Kingdom. (A hermit is a person who does not interact with the rest of the world.)

Opening trade

By the 1800s, China, Japan, and the United States wanted to trade with Korea. Korean leaders said no. Japan attacked Korea in 1876, forcing trade. In 1910 Japan made Korea into a **colony**. From 1910 to 1945, Japan ruled Korea. When Koreans rebelled against harsh Japanese treatment, thousands of people died. Japan continued to rule until its defeat at the end of World War II (1939–1945).

Korean Rulers

2333 BCE–about 108 BCE	Old Joseon Kingdom
57 BCE–668 CE	Three Kingdoms
668–918	Later Silla Dynasty
918–1392	Goryeo Dynasty
1392–1910	Joseon Dynasty
1910–1945	Japanese colony
1945–1948	**Soviet Union** supervision
1948–present	**Dictatorship** under Kim Il Sung/Kim Jong Il

Until 1948, North Korea and South Korea were united under various rulers. Since 1948 North Korea has been an independent country.

A land divided

At the end of World War II, U.S. officials divided Korea along the 38th **parallel**. Troops from the Soviet Union moved into the northern part of Korea. U.S. troops moved into the southern part. In 1946 the Soviets placed Kim Il Sung, a **communist**, in charge of North Korea. Communism is a system in which all people, not individuals, own property. Korea's communist group, the Workers' Party, convinced workers to support Kim.

KIM IL SUNG

(1912–1994)

Kim Il Sung is known as Korea's Great Leader. He was born near Pyongyang. At age 14, he moved to Manchuria with his parents. He became a communist and received military training in the Soviet Union. He became **premier** in 1948 and president in 1972. Kim Il Sung died in 1994 of a heart attack.

Kim Il Sung became premier of North Korea in May 1948, when he was 36 years old.

The Korean War (1950–1953)

Kim Il Sung wanted to unite Korea. He decided to move against South Korea. On June 25, 1950, Kim sent 70,000 troops across the 38th parallel. The northern forces quickly overpowered the poorly trained southern forces. Within a week, the city of Seoul, the capital of South Korea, fell to northern forces. Chinese forces sided with North Korea. The United States supported South Korea. The **United Nations (UN)** sent troops from 15 countries, including the United States, to help South Korea.

On July 27, 1953, North Korea and the United States signed an agreement to stop fighting. They created a **Demilitarized Zone**, called the DMZ, to keep the fighting forces apart. The DMZ still separates North and South Korea.

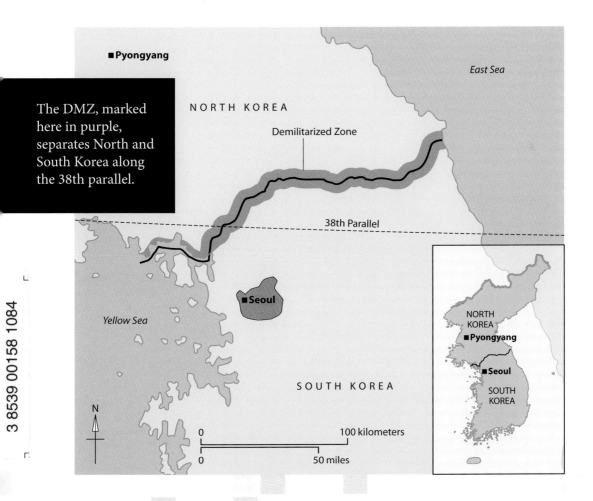

The DMZ, marked here in purple, separates North and South Korea along the 38th parallel.

Pyongyang

East Sea

NORTH KOREA

Demilitarized Zone

38th Parallel

Seoul

Yellow Sea

SOUTH KOREA

N

0   100 kilometers

0   50 miles

NORTH KOREA
Pyongyang
Seoul
SOUTH KOREA

Supportive friends

After the war, millions of North Koreans joined the Communist Party. People who opposed Kim were sent to prison camps or killed. North Korea's **economy** grew rapidly—with help from China and the Soviet Union. However, in the late 1960s, the Soviet Union withdrew support. Today, China continues to support North Korea.

In the 1980s, President Kim Il Sung gave his son, Kim Jong Il, powerful positions within the government. When Kim Il Sung died in 1994, Kim Jong Il became North Korea's leader. Both men shared the goal of uniting North Korea and South Korea under one government. South Korea shares this goal, but neither nation is willing to let the other take control.

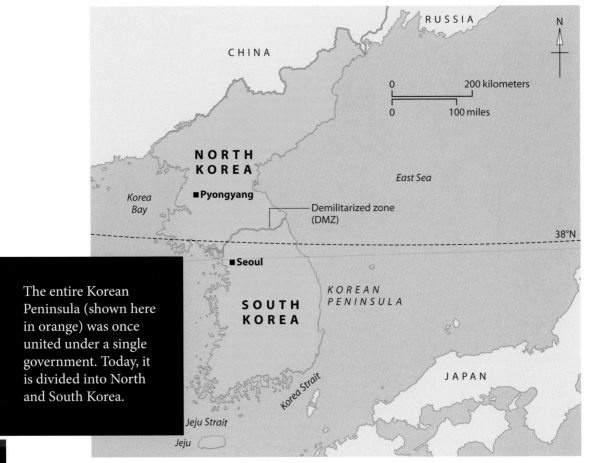

The entire Korean Peninsula (shown here in orange) was once united under a single government. Today, it is divided into North and South Korea.

These North Korean soldiers are guarding the north side of the DMZ, which separates North Korea and South Korea.

Nuclear weapons

North Korea is one of eight countries in the world with nuclear weapons. The United States, China, France, India, Pakistan, Russia, and the United Kingdom also have them. World leaders have urged North Korea to give up its weapons. Sometimes the North Korean government seems ready to agree. Then it changes its mind.

In 2006 South Korea accused North Korea of sinking a warship in waters off the Korean coast. The attack killed 46 South Korean sailors. World leaders worry about what might happen if North Korea decides to use nuclear weapons. In January 2010, North Korean officials hinted that they would give up their weapons in exchange for a peace treaty with South Korea. However, on November 23, 2010, North Korean troops fired artillery rockets at a South Korean island.

Regions and Resources: A Mountainous Land

About 80 percent of North Korea's land is mountainous. Mount Baekdu (also called Paektu), a volcano that is no longer active, is the highest mountain. Deep, narrow valleys separate the mountains. The Amnok and Duman (also called Tuman) rivers form North Korea's northern border with China. North Korea's rivers run west and drain into the Yellow Sea. The rivers cross high mountains, which makes river travel difficult.

Most North Koreans live in the lowland areas. The lowlands make up about 20 percent of North Korea. The widest plains are on the west coast. The coastal plains of Pyongyang and Jaeryong (also called Chaeryong) are each about 310 square miles (500 square kilometers).

A beautiful lake fills the crater of Mount Baekdu, the highest mountain on the Korean Peninsula.

Climate

North Korea has a climate with four seasons: winter, spring, summer, and fall. Winters are long and cold. In January, the coldest month, temperatures range from 36°F (2°C) near the coast to −0.4°F (−18°C) in the mountains. Summers are hot and humid. About 60 percent of the rain falls between June and September. In August average rainfall is 12 inches (317 millimeters). Since the 1990s, North Korea has suffered a series of floods and **droughts** that have caused food shortages.

As this map shows, mountains take up a large portion of North Korea's land.

Daily Life

North Koreans enjoy being outdoors. Ice skating is popular in winter, and fishing is popular in summer. In warm weather, people enjoy hiking in the mountains or running along city paths. City parks have playgrounds for children and cement tables for playing table tennis.

Minerals and mining

Mining is North Korea's most important **industry**. Coal, North Korea's primary energy source, is plentiful. So is magnesium **ore**, a metal used in **manufacturing**. North Korea has about 50 percent of the world's magnesium. Iron ore, zinc, and gold are also mined. A 2001 **UN** study discovered one of the largest gold deposits in the world about 93 miles (150 kilometers) north of Pyongyang. Many countries are eager to buy North Korea's gold. North Korea also has uranium ore deposits. Uranium ore is used to make **nuclear weapons**.

During a power failure, these waiters light candles in a Pyongyang restaurant.

Daily Life

Power outages make daily life difficult. Small towns and villages may have no electricity for days. Even in big city apartments, people use kerosene lanterns or candles for light. Without electricity, there is no hot water, heat, or elevator service. To keep warm, people huddle beneath blankets or light small kerosene stoves.

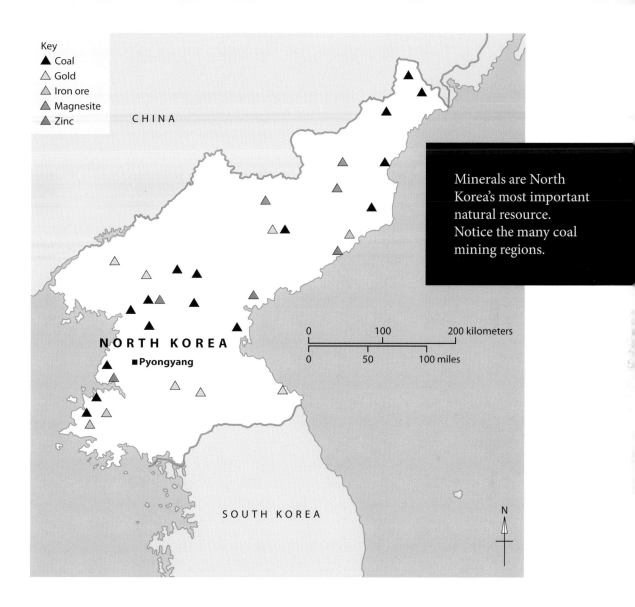

Key
▲ Coal
△ Gold
△ Iron ore
▲ Magnesite
▲ Zinc

CHINA

Minerals are North Korea's most important natural resource. Notice the many coal mining regions.

NORTH KOREA

■Pyongyang

0   100   200 kilometers

0   50   100 miles

SOUTH KOREA

N

Industry

North Korean companies build machines and make military equipment. There are 220 weapon and gun factories, 10 armored vehicle factories, 10 naval shipyards, and 50 ammunition factories. North Korea also builds ships, tanks, and military aircraft for its own use. Since the early 1990s, many factories have been shut down. North Korea does not have the money to repair old factories and aging power plants. When electric power plants fail, schools, factories, and hospitals are left in the dark.

These North Korean workers are unloading food aid in 2008.

Farming and famine

North Korean farms produce rice, corn, potatoes, and soybeans. They raise cattle, pigs, and chickens. However, since the mid-1990s, North Korea has suffered from **famines**. Floods in 1995 and 1996 were followed by a drought in 1997. Between one and two million people died of starvation. Many countries sent food aid.

Food shortages continue to this day. Overuse and flooding damaged farm fields. Today, there is not enough farmland to supply food for everyone. In October 2010, South Korea sent food supplies to North Korea as part of an $8.5 million aid program.

China, North Korea's biggest trading partner, provides about 45 percent of Korea's food. But most Chinese food aid goes to people in the North Korean military. The World Food Program estimates that, in 2010, about one-third of North Koreans did not have enough food to eat.

Transportation

Most North Korean products are moved by train. People also use trains to travel long distances. Few people can afford cars. Even if they could afford them, North Korea has only 466 miles (724 kilometers) of paved roads. Children walk to school, and adults walk to work.

	North Korea	South Korea
Population	22,757,275 (2010 est.)	48,636,068 (2010 est.)
Life expectancy at birth	64.13 years	78.81 years
Per capita income	$1,900 (2009 est.)	$28,100 (2009 est.)
Exports	$2.7 billion (2008)	$432.9 billion (2008 est.)
Imports	$3.6 billion (2008)	$427.3 billion (2008 est.)

North Korean people are often less healthy than South Koreans. Their **economy** is also much weaker. These differences add to the problems between the two countries.

Wildlife: Where Tigers Once Roamed

At one time, tigers, bears, and leopards roamed Korea's forests. Today, many forests have been cut down for lumber and fuel. This leaves many animals with no place to live. Only a few tigers, bears, and deer live in North Korea's mountain forests today.

About 450 **species** of birds have been spotted in Korea. About 50 species live there permanently. Doves, cuckoos, and pheasants are common. Other birds use Korea as a rest stop while migrating to another region.

Plants and flowers

Over 4,500 plant species grow on the Korean **Peninsula**. Roses, irises, and daisies grow in North Korea. So do herbs such as **ginseng**, which is used in medicine. North Korean forests used to have over 900 types of trees. Today, there are still pine and spruce forests in the mountains, but cutting down trees for timber has damaged these forests. Maple, oak, elm and other leaf-bearing trees turn beautiful colors every fall.

Preservation

North Korean scientists want to do more to protect the **environment**. North Korea depends on coal, but coal causes air **pollution**. The overuse of chemicals, farm machinery, and oil has damaged farmlands and waterways. The government tries to raise awareness of the dangers of pollution and the need to save resources. However, at present, the government does not have money to spend on preserving the environment.

National parks

North Korea has several national parks. Most parks honor North Korea's history or leaders. For example, at Mount Myohyang, visitors can see a **Buddhist** temple built in 1042. Nearby, the International Friendship Museum contains 100,000 gifts given to Kim Il Sung by world leaders and admirers.

Tigers, which once roamed North Korea, are extremely rare today.

Infrastructure: Total Control

North Korea is a single-party **communist dictatorship**. This means that the Workers' Party of Korea leads the government. Kim Jong Il leads both the Workers' Party and the People's Army. This makes him the nation's leader. Many people believe that Kim Jong Un, Kim Jong Il's youngest son, will be the next leader. Unlike other communist nations, North Korea passes leadership from father to son.

KIM JONG IL (BORN 1941)

North Korean biographers claim that Kim Jong Il was born on the holy Mount Baekdu. They say that a double rainbow and a star appeared in the sky to mark his birth. He graduated from Kim Il Sung University in 1964, and he became leader after his father, Kim Il Sung, died. North Koreans call him Dear Leader.

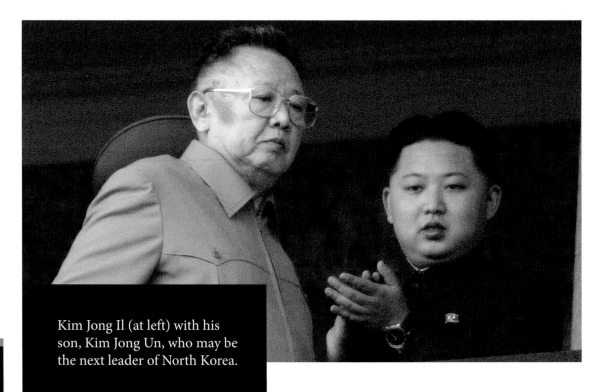

Kim Jong Il (at left) with his son, Kim Jong Un, who may be the next leader of North Korea.

These gymnasts participate in the Arirang Mass Games, which are held for two months every year to celebrate the birthday of Kim Il Sung.

North Korea's **constitution** guarantees freedom of speech, freedom of the press, and freedom of religion. However, these freedoms are limited. For example, the government owns all newspapers and television and radio stations. It is illegal to listen to foreign broadcasts. Internet use is limited. In 2010 North Korea ranked nearly last, or 228 out of 233 countries, in terms of its Internet access.

Health care and other services

The government provides all health care. North Korea is ranked 170 out of 224 nations in terms of **life expectancy**. **Famines**, workplace accidents, and a lack of clean water cause health problems. Current money troubles make it difficult to provide medicine and up-to-date hospital equipment.

Serving the country

North Korea ranks 49th in the world in population, but fourth in military strength. Between one-quarter and one-third of its budget supports the armed forces. About 1.2 million North Koreans serve full-time in the military. Most men join after high school. They must serve for 10 years, or until they reach age 30. Women make up only 5 to 10 percent of the armed forces.

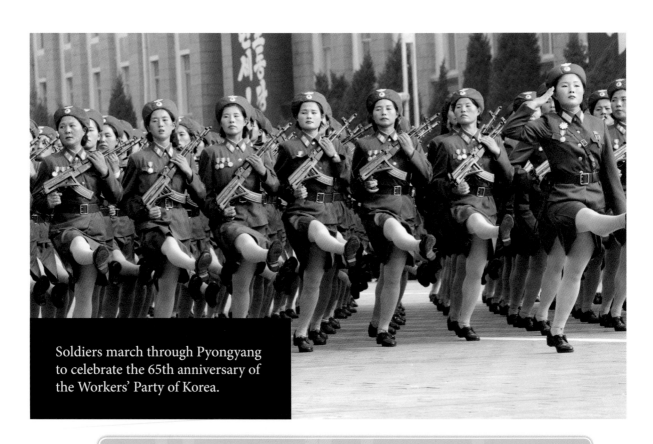

Soldiers march through Pyongyang to celebrate the 65th anniversary of the Workers' Party of Korea.

YOUNG PEOPLE

At age 16, all North Korean students must do volunteer work. Most spend 30 to 40 days doing farmwork during planting time. They spend another 15 to 20 days harvesting crops. Students build highways, monuments, and houses. They work during school vacations and after school. They are not paid for this work.

Daily Life

Most weddings are held on Sundays, when people are not working. The bride and groom bow to Kim Il Sung's picture and then kiss one another. They do not exchange rings. The bride keeps her own name.

This man and woman are celebrating their wedding at the Monument to Party's foundation.

Work units

All North Koreans, from age 6 to 60, belong to something called a work unit. Children belong to work units at school. A father's work unit provides housing, food, clothing, and medical care for his family. A work unit leader is a powerful person. Members of each work unit must get the leader's permission to go to a doctor, travel, marry, or even purchase items such as watches or bicycles.

Education

North Korea has a **literacy rate** of 99 percent. Almost everyone over age 15 can read and write. Schools are free. The government even provides uniforms. Children must attend school for 11 years, beginning with kindergarten. After kindergarten, children attend four years of "people's school." They study the lives of Kim Il Sung and Kim Jong Il, math, and Korean.

These parents are visiting their children's school on the first day of classes.

Daily Life

On school days, students meet their homeroom leader around 7:00 a.m. The children march to school together. Classes begin at 8:00 a.m. They break for lunch at noon. After school, children participate in sports or other group activities.

Children perform for visitors at the Children's Palace.

YOUNG PEOPLE

About 12,000 talented children attend classes in music, dance, **calligraphy**, the martial art **tae kwon do** (also called tae gwon do), and other arts at the Children's Palace in Pyongyang. All art and performances honor North Korea's history or its leaders.

After people's school, children attend six years of senior middle school. Many city schools have 1,000 students. Small villages often share a middle school built for 500 to 600 students. Students continue to study the lives of North Korean leaders and politics. Recently, schools have added computer and English classes.

After graduating, most young women begin working in factories or on farms. They do not choose their own jobs. Rather, jobs are assigned. Most young men begin military training. Very few students go to college. However, a few go to college after they finish military training. Almost no one studies overseas.

Culture: Follow the Leaders

North Korea is an **atheist** state. This means that people do not pray in public or attend places of worship. **Buddhist** temples exist from earlier times. They are now preserved as historic buildings, but they are not used for worship. A few Christian churches exist, but few people attend services. North Koreans do not celebrate religious holidays.

Juche

North Koreans turn to their leaders for guidance. In 1955 Kim Il Sung introduced the idea of *juche*, or self-reliance. The 1972 **constitution** called *juche* the country's guiding principle. *Juche* is a way to encourage farmers, factory workers, and students to work hard to make North Korea a great nation. *Juche* supports the idea that North Koreans should not depend on any other country. It discourages contact with other peoples or nations.

The Juche Tower in Pyongyang, built on the 70th anniversary of Kim Il Sung's birth, reminds the people of North Korea to work toward self-reliance.

Art and literature

Korea has a long tradition of beautiful pottery, painting, and **calligraphy**. Today, however, North Korean art is used for only one purpose: to honor the leaders and the nation. This is true for poetry, nonfiction books, and novels, as well as painting and music. North Koreans read newspapers printed by the government. The Korea Feature Film Studio began producing movies in 1947. Movies honor Kim Il Sung and the Workers' Party. Often Japanese people or Americans are the villains in these films. The North Korean characters are usually good, kind, and loving.

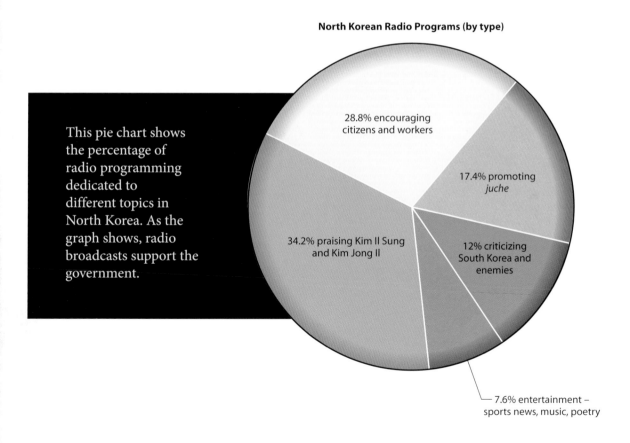

North Korean Radio Programs (by type)

28.8% encouraging citizens and workers

17.4% promoting *juche*

34.2% praising Kim Il Sung and Kim Jong Il

12% criticizing South Korea and enemies

7.6% entertainment – sports news, music, poetry

This pie chart shows the percentage of radio programming dedicated to different topics in North Korea. As the graph shows, radio broadcasts support the government.

Homes

Today, most North Koreans live in apartments in large cities such as Pyongyang, Hamheung (also called Hamhung), and Chongjin (also called Ch'ongjin). Some apartment buildings are 30 to 40 stories high. In the country, Korean homes are usually made of mud bricks. The *ondol* heating system carries heat from the kitchen stove into pipes beneath the floors. Koreans sit and sleep on the warm floors. They never wear shoes inside, but rather leave them at the door.

YOUNG PEOPLE

Between ages 9 and 11, North Korean children join the Young Pioneers. This is the biggest celebration of a child's life. Young Pioneers receive a red scarf and button at a school ceremony held on a national holiday. Parents give presents such as a pen, notebook, or school bag. For two hours a day, Young Pioneers attend training sessions. They learn about their government. Every Saturday, they do volunteer work.

These girls wear the red scarves of the Young Pioneers.

This tall apartment building in Pyongyang is made of cement blocks.

Women in North Korea

North Korean women receive the same school and job opportunities as men. Many women run farms, factories, and have government careers. Women have more responsibilities at home than men do. Old practices continue, however, and men do not always show women equal respect.

YOUNG PEOPLE

Kim Il Sung referred to children as the kings and queens of Korea. They attend well-equipped nursery schools from the age of four months until kindergarten. They play, sing, and dance. Even poor parents find ways to give their children special toys and treats.

Sports

North Korean schools offer a variety of sports, including soccer, basketball, and volleyball. Many students participate in gymnastics. North Korea has several professional soccer teams. Their matches are often televised.

North Korea participates in international sporting events. In the 2008 Summer Olympics in China, North Korean athletes earned six medals, including gold medals in gymnastics and weightlifting. North Korea's soccer team qualified for the 2010 World Cup held in South Africa.

Foods

North Koreans eat rice and vegetables three times a day. *Gimchi* (also called *kimch'i*), a dish made of pickled vegetables such as cabbage or radishes, is served at most meals. Cold noodle dishes are also popular in North Korea. Several city restaurants specialize in noodle dishes. North Koreans often add red and green peppers, soy sauce, onions, garlic, ginger, vinegar, and wine to their food.

North Korea's Jong Tae-se controls the ball during a 2010 match against South Korea in Seoul, South Korea.

Daily Life

Dogs and cats are not considered pets in North Korea. They are not allowed in the cities. Pet stores sell birds and fish as pets. However, only wealthy people can afford them.

Cold sesame noodles

Be sure to have an adult help you make this recipe, especially when boiling the noodles on the stove.

Ingredients

$^1/_4$ lb. naengmyeon noodles (thin noodles made from buckwheat and sweet potato)
2 cups chicken broth
2 cups beef broth, unsalted
1 tbsp. brown rice vinegar
2 tbsp. white vinegar

1 small Asian pear, cut into paper-thin slices
1 egg, hard-boiled and sliced in half
$^1/_2$ Korean cucumber, seeded and then cut into paper-thin slices

What to do

1. Mix the cold broths together with the vinegars.

2. Add more salt or vinegar if desired.

3. Chill in a refrigerator for at least half an hour, if possible.

4. Cook the noodles according to the package directions, about 3 to 5 minutes in boiling water.

5. Drain the noodles and rinse well in cold water. Put the noodles into bowls.

6. Pour a generous amount of chilled broth and a few ice cubes to cover almost all of the noodles.

7. Place half a boiled egg, cucumber slices, and pear slices on top of the noodles.

8. Add ice cubes before serving.

North Korea Today

In many ways, North Korea remains a **hermit** kingdom. Some reports suggest that North Korea's current leader, Kim Jong Il, is not well. His son, Kim Jong Un, may be the next leader. However, other members of Kim's family may take control. Kim Jong Il's sister, Kim Kyong-hui, and his lifelong friend, Choe Ryong-hae, are also possible leaders. Whoever becomes the leader, there are sure to be changes. North Korea's future, like its present, is a mystery.

Much of what we know about North Korea comes from **defectors**, or people who have left North Korea illegally. In 2010 about 18,000 defectors were living in South Korea. Another 30,000 were living in China and Russia.

These high school students, who are defectors from North Korea, attend school in South Korea.

North Korea's Jo Young-Suk won a gold medal in pistol shooting at the 2010 Asian Games. Athletes from Japan and South Korea took 2nd and 3rd place.

YOUNG PEOPLE

At the 2010 Asian Games, athletes from North Korea and South Korea greeted each other and shook hands. They often congratulated one another after a match. However, not everyone acted this way. At the basketball qualifying game, half of the South Korean team members turned their backs when the North Korean national anthem was played.

North Korea has valuable mineral deposits, military power, and educated, hardworking people. Yet, food shortages are a major problem. The threat of war with South Korea is another great concern. Officially, the two countries are still at war. There has never been a peace agreement.

Fact File

Official name: Democratic People's **Republic** of Korea (DPRK)

Nationality: Korean

Official language: Korean

Capital city: Pyongyang

Bordering countries: China (to the north), South Korea (to the south), Russia (to the northeast)

Population: 22,757,275 (July 2010 est.)

Largest cities (populations): Pyongyang (3,171,800)
Hamheung (821,200)
Cheongjin (674,000)
Nampo (655,100)

The won is the currency of North Korea. It is divided into 100 chon.

System of government: Single-party **Communist dictatorship**

Date of independence: August 15, 1945 (from Japan)

Date of constitution: Adopted in 1948; revised in 2009

Official religion: **Atheist**

Life expectancy: 64.13 years

Literacy rate: 99 percent

Area (total): 46,540 square miles (120,538 square kilometers)

Longest river: Amnok, 491 miles (790 kilometers)

Highest elevation: Mount Baekdu, 9,002 feet (2,744 meters)

Lowest elevation: East Sea, 0 feet (0 meters)

Local currency: won

Agricultural products: Rice, corn, potatoes, soybeans, beans; cattle, pigs, pork, eggs

Major industries: Military products, machine building, electric power, chemicals, mining, metallurgy (studying and processing useful metals), textiles, food processing

Imports: Petroleum (oil), coal, machinery and equipment, textiles, grain

Exports: Minerals, metal products, weapons, textiles, agricultural and fishery products

Major markets: China (42 percent), South Korea (38 percent), India (5 percent) (figures are from 2008)

Major suppliers: China (57 percent), South Korea (25 percent), Russia (3 percent), Singapore (3 percent) (figures are from 2008)

National flower: Siebold's Magnolia

Sacred mountain: Mount Baekdu

Emblem: A hydroelectric (water) power plant under Mount Baekdu, in the light of a five-pointed red star with ears of rice forming a frame

Famous North Koreans: Dangun, founder of the Korean nation
Hong Un Jong (born 1989), gold medalist in the 2008
  Olympics for the women's vault competition
Kim Il Sung (1912–1994), first president of DPRK
Kim Jong Il (born 1941), current leader of DPRK
Pak Hyon Suk (born 1985), gold medalist in the 2008
  Olympics in women's weightlifting

National holidays:

January 1	New Year's Day
First day of first lunar month	Korean New Year
February 16	Kim Jong Il's Birthday
April 15	Kim Il Sung's Birthday
April 25	Army Day
May 1	Workers' Day
July 27	Victory Day
September 9	Founding of DPRK
October 10	Workers' Party of Korea Day
December 27	Constitution Day

National anthem
"Aegukka" ("Let Morning Shine")

Let morning shine on the silver and gold of this land,
Three thousand leagues packed with natural wealth.
My beautiful fatherland.
The glory of a wise people
Brought up in a culture brilliant
With a history five millennia long.
Let us devote our bodies and minds
To supporting this Korea forever.

In cities, most people travel on foot or in tramcars such as the ones shown here.

Timeline

BCE means Before the Common Era. When this appears after a date, it refers to the number of years before the Christian religion began. BCE dates are always counted backward.

CE means Common Era. When this appears after a date, it refers to the time after the Christian religion began.

BCE

28,000	Ancient people live on the Korean **Peninsula**.
3000	**Ancestors** of modern Korean people move to the Korean Peninsula from Asia.
2333	Dangun founds the Old Joseon Kingdom.
108	China conquers the northern part of Korea.
57	The kingdoms of Goguryeo, Silla, and Baekje are formed.

CE

300s	The Goguryeo Kingdom becomes **Buddhist**.
668	Korea is **unified** under the Silla Kingdom.
935	Wang Geon (also called Wang Kon), founder of the Goryeo **Dynasty**, rules Korea.
1231	The Mongols invade Korea.
1392	Yi Seonggye (also called Yi Songgye), founder of the new Joseon Dynasty, becomes ruler of Korea.
1446	The Korean alphabet is invented.
1600s	The Manchus invade Korea.
1876	Japan forces Korea to become a trading partner.
1910	Japan claims Korea as a **colony**.

1945	Korea is divided into two by the United States and the **Soviet Union**.
1948	Kim Il Sung becomes **premier** of the Democratic People's **Republic** of Korea.
1950	North Korea invades South Korea. The Korean War begins.
1953	A truce (agreement) ends active fighting in the Korean War.
1990s	**Famine** kills thousands.
1994	Kim Il Sung dies.
1997	Kim Jong Il becomes premier.
2000	Leaders of North and South Korea meet for the first time.
2006	North Korea conducts a test of **nuclear weapons**.
2007	Passenger trains cross the North–South border for the first time in 56 years.
2010	Kim Jong Il appoints his youngest son, Kim Jong Un, to important political and military jobs.

Glossary

ancestor person from whom an individual is descended; someone more distant than a grandparent

artificial human-made; not natural

atheist person or government that denies or disbelieves the existence of a supreme being (a god) or beings

BCE meaning "before the common era." When this appears after a date, it refers to the time before the Christian religion began. BCE dates are always counted backward.

Buddhist of the religion Buddhism, originated in India by Buddha (Siddhartha Gautama)

calligraphy beautiful penmanship, especially highly decorative handwriting

CE meaning "common era." When this appears after a date, it refers to the time after the Christian religion began.

colony area ruled by another country

communist person or country that practices a social system in which all people share work and property

constitution system of laws and principles that govern a nation, state, or corporation

culture practices, beliefs, and traditions of a society

defector person who has left North Korea illegally

Demilitarized Zone (DMZ) artificial boundary between North and South Korea about 2.5 miles (4 kilometers) wide, designed to keep their fighting forces separated

dictatorship government by one ruler who has absolute power over the people

drought period of dry weather that damages crops

dynasty series of rulers from the same family or group

economy having to do with the money, industries, and jobs in a country

environment natural world, including plants and animals

export to ship goods to other countries for sale or exchange

famine extreme shortage of food

ginseng herb used in medicine

hermit person who does not interact with the rest of the world

import to bring in from a foreign country for use or sale

industry general business activity or trade

isolated separated from other persons or things; alone

life expectancy average number of years of life for a group of individuals

literacy rate number of adults over the age of 15 who can read and write

manufacturing making or producing a product by hand or by using machinery

nuclear weapon missile or bomb that uses energy made by splitting atoms

ore mineral in the ground that contains metal valuable enough to be mined

parallel any of the imaginary lines equidistant from the equator and representing degrees of latitude on Earth's surface

peninsula land area almost completely surrounded by water and connected to the mainland by a narrow strip of land

pollution addition of harmful gases or chemicals to the environment, for example, to the air or water

premier leader of a country

republic independent country with a head of government who is not a king or queen

Soviet Union former union of 15 republics in Eastern Europe and Asia that ended in 1991

species particular type of animal or plant

tae kwon do Korean martial art used in self-defense

unify to make into a single unit

United Nations (UN) international organization formed in 1945 to promote world peace

Find Out More

Books

Gifford, Clive. *North Korea (Global Hotspots)*. New York: Marshall Cavendish Benchmark, 2010.

Piddock, Charles. *North Korea (Nations in the News)*. Milwaukee: World Almanac Library, 2007.

Santella, Andrew. *The Korean War (We the People)*. Minneapolis: Compass Point, 2007.

Websites

https://www.cia.gov/library/publications/the-world-factbook/index.html
Find out more by reading the CIA World Factbook entry on North Korea.

www.korea-dpr.com/
Visit North Korea's official website.

www.nationalanthems.info/kp.htm
Listen to North Korea's national anthem.

www.indiana.edu/~koreanrs/hangul.html
Learn more about the Korean language at this website.

news.bbc.co.uk/2/hi/asia-pacific/country_profiles/1131421.stm
Find out about North Korea on the BBC's website.

travel.nationalgeographic.com/travel/countries/north-korea-facts/
North Korea facts can be found on this website.

Places to visit

Most Americans will not be allowed to visit North Korea because the United States is considered an enemy. However, the following U.S. museums have large collections of Korean art:

Asian Art Museum, Chong-Moon Lee Center for Asian Art and Culture, San Francisco, California

www.asianart.org/index.html

The Asian Art Museum is one of the largest museums in the Western world devoted to Asian arts. Special family programs give children a look at the arts and festivals of Asia, including Korea.

Korean Cultural Center of Los Angeles

www.kccla.org/english_/home_.asp

The Korean Cultural Center of Los Angeles welcomes the public to experience the rich history and culture of Korea. They hold special programs and events.

Korean Cultural Service of New York

www.koreanculture.org/?mid=main

The Korean Cultural Service of New York provides activities related to Korean culture including gallery exhibitions, performing arts concerts, film festivals, and educational programs.

Topic Tools

You can use these topic tools for your school projects. Trace the flag and map on to a sheet of paper, using the thick black outlines to guide you, then color in your pictures. Make sure you use the right colors for the flag!

North Korea's flag was created in 1948. White is a traditional color of Korea. The white bands stand for purity, strength, and dignity. The blue stripes represent North Korea's desire for peace. The red shows that the country is communist. The star represents the Workers' Party of Korea.

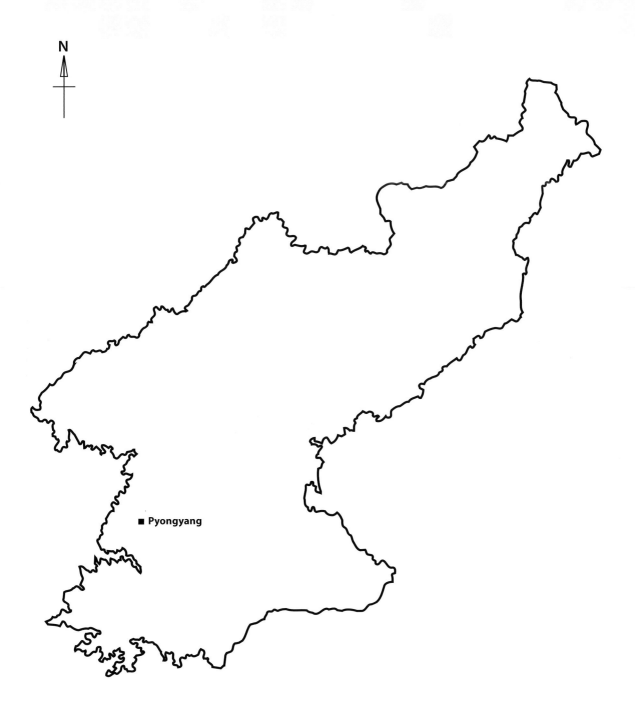

Index

Titles in the series

Afghanistan	978 1 4329 5195 5
Algeria	978 1 4329 6093 3
Australia	978 1 4329 6094 0
Brazil	978 1 4329 5196 2
Canada	978 1 4329 6095 7
Chile	978 1 4329 5197 9
China	978 1 4329 6096 4
Costa Rica	978 1 4329 5198 6
Cuba	978 1 4329 5199 3
Czech Republic	978 1 4329 5200 6
Egypt	978 1 4329 6097 1
England	978 1 4329 5201 3
Estonia	978 1 4329 5202 0
France	978 1 4329 5203 7
Germany	978 1 4329 5204 4
Greece	978 1 4329 6098 8
Haiti	978 1 4329 5205 1
Hungary	978 1 4329 5206 8
Iceland	978 1 4329 6099 5
India	978 1 4329 5207 5
Iran	978 1 4329 5208 2
Iraq	978 1 4329 5209 9
Ireland	978 1 4329 6100 8
Israel	978 1 4329 6101 5
Italy	978 1 4329 5210 5
Japan	978 1 4329 6102 2
Latvia	978 1 4329 5211 2
Liberia	978 1 4329 6103 9
Libya	978 1 4329 6104 6
Lithuania	978 1 4329 5212 9
Mexico	978 1 4329 5213 6
Morocco	978 1 4329 6105 3
New Zealand	978 1 4329 6106 0
North Korea	978 1 4329 6107 7
Pakistan	978 1 4329 5214 3
Philippines	978 1 4329 6108 4
Poland	978 1 4329 5215 0
Portugal	978 1 4329 6109 1
Russia	978 1 4329 6110 7
Scotland	978 1 4329 5216 7
South Africa	978 1 4329 6112 1
South Korea	978 1 4329 6113 8
Spain	978 1 4329 6111 4
Tunisia	978 1 4329 6114 5
United States of America	978 1 4329 6115 2
Vietnam	978 1 4329 6116 9
Wales	978 1 4329 5217 4
Yemen	978 1 4329 5218 1